Gary Jackson

WORKOUT

EXERCISES AT

HOME

The Beginner's Step-by-Step Guide to Doing Exercises at Home without Equipment for a Perfect Body and Healthy Life.

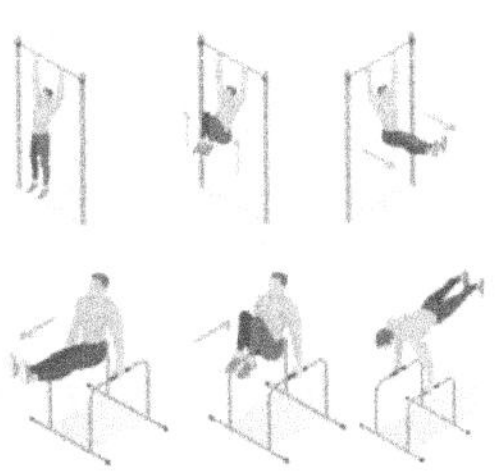

© Copyright 2021 by **Gary Jackson**

Gary Jackson

© Copyright 2021 by Gary Jackson - **All rights reserved**.

Gary Jackson

Table of Contents

3

Gary Jackson

CHAPTER 1 – Breath and Stretch

Anyone who was not a fitness buff before quarantine does not become one now. Here is how to fight back and neck pain caused by forced sedentariness, with easy breathing and stretching exercises.

The many workouts and circuits to do at home that are offered online are not for everyone. If you were not a sportsman before the epidemic, it is hard to be a sportsman now. On the contrary: squats, lunges, and jumps, if done badly and without the precautions that fitness enthusiasts know well, they risk becoming counterproductive. In short, the sedentary in this period of forced isolation are even more exposed to neck and back pain, also because of the many hours spent between sofa, chair, and improvised workstations, perhaps shared with children and life companions. To feel better and recover some well-being, there are, however, some simple daily actions that everyone can perform, based on breathing and stretching.

Apnea

Why call in the apnea? Because - explain the experts - breathing is the basis of everything and it is important to know it to perform even the simplest of wellness exercises, such as stretching. Knowing the basics of breathing is essential to loosen contractures and help the muscles to stretch. But it is also useful to rebalance the body, strengthen it and increase its energy capacity. We do not realize it but most of us have "high" breathing, i.e. we do not use the diaphragm well, and fast. Note that while you are at your desk or standing on the phone, your shoulders are probably raised, close to your ears and closed in. Now, this is the classic position that at the end of the day causes pain in the base of the neck and upper back. And those who are often like this usually breathe badly, i.e. quickly and with the upper part of the diaphragm".

If we learn the techniques to breathe well, we can succeed, in addition to reducing cervical and back pain, in controlling part of the anxiety we are experiencing at the moment. These techniques can be adopted in any situation and position: standing, sitting, cooking, working at the PC, in the shower. The execution time must be a couple of minutes per exercise, to be repeated several times a day. Let us start with breathing.

5 exercises to breathe well

Breathing consists of four phases: inhalation, exhalation, exhalation and apnea. Being aware of this is important to manage it in the best possible way.

1. Inhale

Let us start with the management of inhalation through the nose: mentally count 4 seconds and then always exhale through the nose for another 4 seconds. We can increase the difficulty of the first exercise by lengthening the expiratory time to 6-8 seconds.

2. You are in apnea

At this point we insert a phase of inspiratory apnea: after having done our inhalation with the nose, we hold our breath for at least 3 seconds and then exhale with the mouth.

3. Inhale, exhale and then hold your breath.

Now let us go create an expiratory apnea phase. We always start with our inhalation from the nose followed immediately by the next expiratory phase, and then perform an expiratory apnea: it is simply to hold the breath for 3 seconds and then take it again. They may perhaps seem too simple and useless exercises but, on the contrary, the usefulness of complete breathing is essential to access the subsequent phases of muscle work and, if desired, aerobic work.

4. Breathe in, breathe out, apnea

In the fourth exercise we will insert both the inspiratory and expiratory apnea phases: we always start by inhaling through the nose for 4 seconds, hold the breath for 3 seconds and exhale 4-8 seconds, then hold the breath for another 3 seconds and repeat.

5. Inhale, apnea, exhale, apnea, exhale

With the fifth exercise we also include exhalation in our process: after completing the inhalation phase with the nose you have to exhale with the mouth and conclude by exhaling. This also serves to recall the deep muscles.

5 stretching exercises for back, neck and legs

Now let us move on to the "dynamic" phase to add to the breathing. In practice, a few movements of legs and arms are combined with correct breathing: simple moves to avoid back pain, especially in the lumbar area, or in the neck and shoulders.

1. Open and close your arms

Let's start with the upper part of the body: inhaling we open our arms in front of us, extending them outwards as far as possible and keeping them at shoulder height, which must be lowered and not contracted; exhaling we close them in front of us.

2. Extend your arms above your head and then lower them.

The second exercise always starts with an inhalation that leads us this time to stretch our arms above our heads for 15 seconds, then exhale and lower our arms simultaneously.

3. Touch your toes

The third exercise involves stretching the back chain of the legs: you have to go down to touch our toes with a long, gentle exhalation. Try stretching with each exhalation and you will see the results.

4. Rotate your torso

Now let us prepare ourselves to small rotations of the torso: with our hands on our hips, we go towards the right-side inhaling and then exhale and reposition ourselves centrally. Then we perform the same movement to the left.

5. Extend your arms above your head and touch your toes.

To conclude, the complete execution of an inhalation by stretching the arms above the head, and then exhale reaching as far as possible towards the tip of the feet.

14

CHAPTER 2 – Daily Home Exercises

As mentioned earlier, quarantined home exercises are the only chance we have to keep fit.

But if smart working is the new office, what about the sport and training that were the rule to stay fit before the emergency?

Many people have voted for fitness apps and tutorials on YouTube, live on Facebook and Instagram, but who does not have time (or desire) to carve out (at least) half an hour to train, what should they do?

That's why we have developed a special training program: a real smart workout, to be put into practice in smart working time, ideal to keep fit if you have no way to follow a complete program but want to keep moving.

In our daily schedule, short workout sessions are inserted between an email and a call. Or you can do them while you wait for the pasta water to boil.

They are simple and affordable exercises that are done regularly but keep the body active and the mind efficient. Try it to believe.

Exercises to do in bed to reactivate the body

A few minutes to open your eyes and get used to the light of the new day and immediately some gentle gymnastics to wake your body.

You will love these exercises to do in bed, in the warm embrace of the blankets.

It only takes a few minutes to do: six twists of the torso to the right and left; ten circumduction of the wrists and ankles to reactivate the circulation of the extremities; three deep, complete breaths (inhaling through the nose, first swell the belly and then the chest; exhaling slowly through the mouth, first deflate the chest and then the abdomen).

Pass in a sitting position on the bed and make some head movements back and forth, left, and right. Now put your feet and all your toes on the floor and push from your heels, stand up and sit down for about ten times as if you were doing a squat (in the sweet awakening version) to stretch your knees and give a twist to your legs.

Exercises to do while working against sedentariness

After breakfast, off to smart working day!

In the office as well as at home, the expert rule applies that to feel good you have to get up from your chair at least every half hour. If you have to give up the coffee break with colleagues or the classic two steps in the courtyard, in the total freedom of your home here are the exercises to do between emails (if only to avoid that the destination is every time the refrigerator).

Simply stand up, contract, and relax your buttocks ten times.

Always in an upright position, with your arms along your hips, bring your arms up above your head and down (no-stop fifteen times). For a more sprint variant, do the same exercise but jump (aka jumping jacks).

The short session continues with ten squats that are good for the buttocks, biceps femoral and quadriceps. Here is how: from the upright position, bring your hips back, bending your knees and lowering your torso keeping it straight, without ever bending your back, and then return to the upright position. And to finish one minute of plank.

And now, time's up, time to get back to work!

Making the stairs at home to tone the buttocks.

After eating you will be remotely connected, your colleagues, perhaps a call conference during which it is strongly discouraged to nod off. To avoid this, after you have set up the kitchen and before returning to your station, get going.

If you live in an apartment building, leave the apartment, and walk up the stairs quickly from the first to the top floor. If you do not have any plans to climb, take a few minutes of steps: just one step from which to climb and descend repeatedly first with one foot and then with the other.

More demanding exercises to firm the entire body

To break up the day, do 5-10 push-ups on the floor (also useful to dilute the tension that has grown in you after reading the last email of fire from your boss); do about ten frontal lunges for each leg that help to re-establish the centre of gravity and then, ideally, to regain the focus on yourself (this applies to all the exercises where balance and coordination are required).

For frontal lunges, from an upright position, bend your left leg downwards to form a right angle, stopping before touching the floor with your knee. The right leg bends accordingly. Return to the starting position by pushing with your front foot.

One minute of exercise to relieve tension and increase metabolism

If you realize in the afternoon that you are losing sprint and concentration, nothing helps more (except a triple coffee) than a high ski session.

Here is how: from the upright position, bend your knees and bring them towards your chest, alternating left and right legs. Repeat the movement 20 times or if you can for one minute.

Do this several times a day and your metabolism will benefit.

Relaxing exercises: yoga, stretching and meditation

After a day like this, between work and fitness, where you have climbed condos, done push-ups, skips and squats, do you want to train again?

Our advice is to end the day with some yoga or stretching and a meditation session.

For those who have never practiced yoga before, you can start by saying goodbye to the sun. But simple stretching exercises for the back and legs are also good, perhaps done with more attention and more concentration than you usually put in after the normal training session in the gym.

More advanced yogis can indulge in their usual practice: a vinyasa to reconnect and unite body, mind, and breath; a sequence of asanas to release tension in the neck, shoulders and back.

And to close, a little meditation. Choose a corner of the house that seems suitable to you, place a couple of pillows on the floor or on the mat, sit in a comfortable position with your eyes closed, with your inner gaze pointing straight to the horizon, start breathing.

Listen to the air coming in and out of your nostrils gradually becoming an increasingly regular, constant, controlled flow. As this happens, relax your body where you feel tension and empty your mind of thoughts.

Those who have been meditating for a long time and know the different techniques of pranayama can take advantage of these moments to dedicate themselves to their individual practice.

For those who start now, it is an opportunity to discover and experience new ways of feeling. It must be said that it does not matter how much you stand still and "alone with yourself" on the mat, it matters how much intensity and dedication you experience the moment. And in the end, psycho-physical well-being is guaranteed.

CHAPTER 3 – Exercises For Free Body

Just one rule: have the constancy to do them (almost) every day. This is just 15 minutes total (one minute per exercise with 30 seconds between each one).

Squat for buttocks and thighs

A classic that never goes out of fashion and that, after the inevitable pain after training, really gives great satisfaction is the squat.

They are performed freehand or with a weight in your hands, keeping your feet slightly wider than your hips and firmly on the ground.

Ascent and descent must be controlled so that the knees do not exceed the foot line and the torso does not fall too far forward or too far back.

If the buttocks contract and squat well on the way up, the effectiveness of the squats increases.

Frontal lunges for legs and buttocks

In addition to training the buttocks, the lunges work all over the leg and improve balance.

For the more experienced there is the version of the jumped lunges, but for those who are impractical or are at the beginning it is always better to control well every single movement and perform the exercise in static.

As for squats, also in this case the knee must not exceed the foot line but form a 90° angle.

Half arch for back and buttocks

For those who dream of a marble B-side this is the ideal exercise!

It has no contraindications; it is practiced in the drain and therefore without the risk of compromising the knees.

Beware only of those who suffer from pain in the cervical area: in that case it is good to take care not to overload the neck too much.

To avoid discomfort, simply reduce the width of the riser.

Table to strengthen arms, back and buttocks

A complete but somewhat hard exercise that completes the series of squats, frontal lunges and bows and adds the load on the arms.

You may find it hard to hold the position at first, but with time the resistance increases.

The ideal is to be able to stay in the table position for 30 seconds, loosen and recover for 15 seconds and then try again for at least three or four consecutive repetitions.

If well done, fatigue, results and strength are assured!

Basic side abs

A simple exercise to train the side abs consists of bending over on one side and then on the other in an alternating direction.

The effectiveness of the exercise increases if you hold weights in your hands (which in the absence of the classic gym dumbbells can be replaced by water bottles or other easily grip able objects).

Front plate for iron abdominals

Sculpted abs do not just mean flat tummies, but also a well straight torso and better posture.

The frontal plank is the ideal exercise to achieve this goal and not only: in addition to the abdominal core, the muscles of the legs are also trained during tightness, which must remain well contracted in order to support the weight of the body in the best possible way.

Just be careful not to arch your back, especially during the last few seconds of tightness.

Lateral Plank

After the frontal plank to complete the abdominal workout perform a few repetitions of lateral plank never fails!

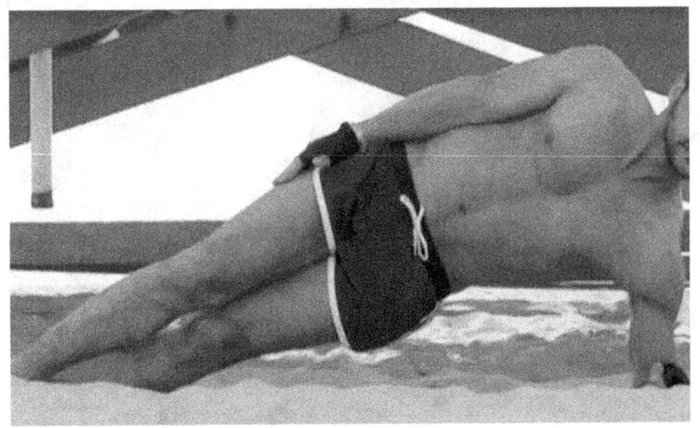

All lateral leg and torso muscles are involved in this exercise and the hold on the arm also produces a training effect on the shoulder and arm.

Twist to train mobility, strength, and abdominal endurance

A complete exercise for those who aim to have a super sculpted turtle.

The exercise is performed with or without the addition of a weight or ball in the hands and consists of rotating the torso from one side and then the other while the legs are raised off the ground.

It will burn a lot, but the combined action of holding the legs up and twist will have an exponential effect on the definition of the abs!

Spines and back

To be fit and perform all the exercises well you need a strong back.

One of the most effective exercises to train the large back (and reflex arms and shoulders) are the backward lifts, to be performed in quadrupeds or in support of a raised surface.

During the execution, the back should be kept straight, and the exercise should focus only on the portion of muscle concerned, i.e. the back.

Burpee

The burpees are the functional free-body exercise preferred by Americans.

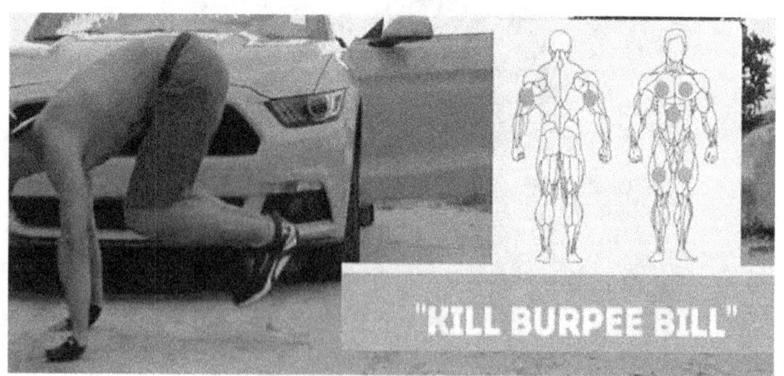

As complete as it is exhausting, it is an extremely dynamic movement that combines action, strength, coordination with a truly remarkable cardio-vascular and cardio-respiratory commitment.

There are various ways to perform it, in all cases it is to get down to the ground with a squat, put your hands on the ground and bring your legs back with a jump, at that point do a bend, another jump to bring your feet closer to your hands and finally a high jump to get back on your feet.

How to train your arms

Stand supine on your knees with your legs together. Place your hands sideways at a slightly greater distance from your shoulders and bend your arms. Inhale and keep your body aligned, contract the buttocks and abdomen, and stretch your arms. Then, exhale and return to the starting position. Repeat for at least 10 times. Execute 3 series, taking a minute break between each series. The advantages? This exercise strengthens the upper body, especially the triceps.

How to make your belly more toned

Stand with your legs apart at the same shoulder width. Bend your knees and torso forward slightly and place your palms between your feet on the ground. Leveraging the palms of your hands, with the arms outstretched, bring your right foot back resting only the tip on the ground and stretch the corresponding leg. Then bring back your left foot. Return to the starting position by first bringing the right foot forward and then the left foot. Repeat the exercise 15 times. Do 3 sets, with a one-minute stop between sets.

How to firm your legs

Stand with your legs outstretched and your feet apart, slightly further apart than your shoulders and your toes out. Place a stack of books behind you four fingers lower than your knees. Bend your legs and come down slowly with your pelvis until you touch the stack with your buttocks. Pause for 3 seconds, without sitting down, pushing your knees out. Then slowly spread your legs and return to the starting position. Repeat the exercise 10 times. Do 3 sets, with a one-minute break between sets.

Gary Jackson

CHAPTER 4 – Keep Fit Without Diets

Staying at home, without a gym, going out in the evening or even just the journeys to and from work, however, risks being detrimental to your physical fitness, because you tend to eat more (and badly) for boredom and consume much less.

To overcome the problem, without staying on a quarantine diet because it is not that you can really ruin your life, there are some tricks that will allow you not to gain weight and maintain muscle tone.

Eating seasonal food helps the immune system

Buying seasonal fruit and vegetables allows you to choose from a wide variety of raw materials grown locally, and this makes it, as well as much cheaper, less impacting on the planet, much better and above all much richer in all those nutrients and vitamins that at this time more than ever are needed by the body to maintain a high level of protection of the immune system.

Optimize the ingredients and buy different foods than usual.

When you go shopping, try to imagine which dishes you will want to cook during the week. And imagine more uses depending on the deadline: by buying potatoes, for example, you can cook them as a side dish, make a mash, a velvet or even bake them in the oven together with onion, sour cream and bacon: a real treat.

All of us have a more or less fixed budget that we repeat almost helplessly week after week, ending up eating the same things over and over again.

A very simple way to vary a little bit is to be inspired by the products that almost all supermarkets alternate in promotion. Is there bacon? How long has it been since you have had a carbonara?

Using colour-contrasting dishes helps to eat less

A study conducted by Cornell University's Food and Brand Lab has shown that when there is little colour contrast between food and dish, there is a tendency to serve up to

30% more food than when the colour of the dish and the colour of the food are very different.

So, if you decide to eat a plate of tomato pasta, choose a light-coloured one when you want to serve something clear.

Using smaller plates makes us feel full first

Again, this is optical illusion.

If we use large plates or with a very wide base, like flat ones, the contents will look poor and we will tend to put more food to fill the space.

On the contrary, in front of a smaller plate full of food we will feel like we are eating more.

Research published in the American Journal of Preventative Medicine showed that when participants were given a larger bowl, they served 31% more ice cream than those who were given a smaller bowl.

You don't need to buy a new set of dishes, just use fruit plates, for example.

Turn off the television and shut off your mobile phone.

Right now, we are all constantly looking for new information and bombarded by numbers, news and hoaxes from social media, newspapers, TV, and chat.

Here, define at least a few hours a day to give it a rest: turn everything off and talk about something else, anything other than the coronavirus.

This will be good for both your spirit and your waist, because it has been shown that eating in front of the TV on or with the phone in your hand is not only a problem for conversation, but also for your diet.

An English study has shown that eating while distracted induces you to eat more, both at the table and after meals.

This is because the body - especially the brain - is not concentrated in the main activity and therefore does not perceive well the stimulus and awareness of having ingested enough food.

Do sport at home

Forget about giving up at the table, the real secret of any good fitness is movement. And it is not necessarily that it cannot be done even within the four walls of the house.

CHAPTER 5 – Pair workout

Training as a couple is a great way to make some exercises even more effective, because we help each other, to strengthen the bonds with the partner or friend with whom we train with us.

Couple training allows us to enhance the effectiveness of exercises, such as stretching exercises. With a little help, we can stretch our leg muscles even more and hold the position at full strength for longer.

In addition, there are many benefits in relational terms. Being together during training allows us to share and strengthen relationships with the other person. If we train with our partner, this will be the best way to spend time together and practice something important for yourself.

If we are a bit lazy, organising a workout together can increase our motivation. Training as a couple can also be done with a friend of ours and we can decide together with her on specific goals to pursue together.

Couple Workout

Doing a nice workout for two is more fun and with the right exercises you can train together, not just at the same time. In this article we propose a perfect workout program for you to do in pairs.

Pair workouts are training sessions in which you train with a partner. When you train alone, you do the exercises one after the other, but in this type of workout, you can "use" your partner as support or to make the exercise more difficult.

Partner workouts are more fun, and, with a little imagination, you will be able to expand the range of exercises and stimulate your muscles in new ways. In addition to strength and endurance, you learn to feel your body differently.

By training in two, you have to continually adapt your movements to the person in front of you and this improves coordination and increases self-confidence.

When you tackle new exercises, it is advisable to perform the movements slowly at first. For example, in the tuck jump you should both feel confident. You have to be sure that you can jump on your partner, the other person has to trust that you will not fall on her. The same goes for the other exercises.

Here are some rather simple exercises that you can perform in pairs.

Push-ups

The push-ups are done in pairs like this: lie on the floor on your stomach. The partner will have to do the same but above us, keeping his arms crossed at the height of our neck. Do the push-ups on top of each other, as many as you can and exchange the position to rest?

Walking on the arms

It's also called a walk on the arms. This exercise serves to strengthen the muscles of the arms. The exercise is done in this way: lie down on the floor with your stomach down. The partner takes our legs by pulling them up and tightening them on his hips.

In this position you start by walking forward on your arms only. With this training you strengthen your biceps, triceps, and pecs.

Squat

It's an easy exercise: stand in front of each other and perform a squat downwards, holding your hands with your arms crossed. This exercise is useful for toning the legs and buttocks.

Side plank with rotation and applause

Get in the side plank position, back to back. You start by supporting yourself with your right arm and keeping your feet together and your abs contracted, then raise your left arm up, perpendicular to the ground, to form a "T". Your partner places himself in the same position as you, but on the other side and with his right arm raised. From this position, rotate on your back (backwards, upwards) to give you a five and then on your belly (forwards, downwards) to give you another five. A repetition includes two applause. Do 8-12 and then change sides.

Isometric squat and run knee-high on the spot

In this case everyone plays his part, but it is to be done in pairs because the exercise of one depends on the other. While you count

100 knees up, your partner stays in isometric squat, then you take over. Repeat both exercises 5 times each.

Push up and tap alternately

Facing each other, get in the plank position. Simultaneously push up and climb. At this point, you with your right hand touch your partner's left shoulder and simultaneously your partner touches your left shoulder with his right hand. Continue 8-12 times alternating arms.

Give me a 5 in plank

As in the previous year, start from the plank position, face to face. From this position, lift the opposite arm and give yourself a five and then return with both hands to the ground and give yourself a five with the other hand. There should be no downtime: as soon as you put your hand back on the ground, raise the other arm immediately. Do as many repetitions as possible in 30 seconds.

Squat jump with applause

Stand next to each other but turn in the opposite direction, half a metre apart. Go down in squats and jump at the same time. In the flight phase, high-five with the hand on the side next to your partner. There are no breaks between squats, so do 8-12 squat jumps with applause and then change sides.

Partner Pistol Squat

Trust is essential here because you will make a squat gun with the support of your partner.

Face each other and hold on to your forearms. Both of you put your weight on your left leg and lift your right foot then start to descend slowly by bending your elbows a little. Bend your support leg and keep your abs and back straight. Descend as far down as possible without losing the position then climb up naturally holding on to the other. Be careful not to rely on him alone, you still have to keep your support leg strong.

Plank and jump

Again, you will do two different but related exercises. One is in a plank position, with your back straight and your abs contracted. The other one stands next to the ankles of the first one and makes lateral jumps using the body of the partner as an obstacle. Between jumps there are no breaks: as soon as you land, you jump immediately in the opposite direction to train the explosive force. In 30 seconds, you have to do as many jumps as possible, then you reverse the roles.

To increase the difficulty, those who are not jumping can switch from plank to bench position several times during the 30 seconds, thus varying the height of the obstacle for their partner.

Pedalling in pairs

Another great exercise to tone and firm the legs to be done together with a friend or partner is to make a kind of "exercise bike" in the air, pushing each other's legs.

Lie down on the floor, join the soles of your feet, and start practicing the movement as if you were lying on a bicycle.

Keep your arms perpendicular to your body, lie on the floor and contract your abs well. Repeat the exercise several times for a couple of minutes.

With these simple exercises to be done in pairs, training for perfect physical fitness will certainly be more fun. What are you waiting for? Get your partner involved and start training.

Gary Jackson

58

CONCLUSION

Thank you for coming all the way to the end of this book, we hope it was informative and able to provide you with all the tools you need to achieve your goals, whatever they may be.

This book has tried to bring all the important points to the fore so that you can get all the benefits without having to deal with the negative effects.

All you must do is follow the information provided in the book and follow the directions.

You can also get all the benefits of the process by following the simple steps in the book.

I hope this book will really help you achieve your goals.

Gary Jackson

www.ingramcontent.com/pod-product-compliance
Lightning Source LLC
Chambersburg PA
CBHW061055050726
47592CB00004B/1689